Lightin Up!

Lightin Up!

Healing Through Passion and Humor

SECOND EDITION

Art Hochberg

A Dr. Art Book

Kalima Publishing, Philadelphia, Pennsylvania

Library of Congress Control Number: 2012950233

Lightin Up!: Healing Through Passion and Humor, Second Edition
Art Hochberg, Kalima Publishing, 2013
p. cm.
Trade paperback
ISBN 13: 978-0-9859450-3-9
1. Self-Help. 2. Existential Psychology. 3. Spirituality. 4. Wisdom. 5. Healing.

"A Dr. Art Book"

His friends call him "Dr. Art." With incisive wit and style of a Zen master the good doctor offers patience, gratitude and the determination to be all right with our selves. **Lightin Up!** is a potent remedy for hopelessness and despair.

Trade eBook ISBN: 978-0-9859450-5-3

First published 2012.

Cover Design and Graphics by Didona Design Associates.
Ebook Publication and Conversion by YourPubtoEpub.com.
Illustrations by Brian Hainstock.
Dr. Art, "Letting Go!" photo by Greg Robinson.

Dedicated to

M. R. Bawa Muhaiyaddeen

A genuine Sufi Master

Table of Contents

The World Isn't What You Think

The work? It's wherever we are at. Staying in that place is a successful life. We already have a successful life. This is why we came here! And, you know what? To realize that we are here is to realize that that we are alive here now, and that's all that counts.

The work does not have to be done alone. This is the secret to success to let each scene come to us to be open to change. All change comes from within us. It does not come from the outside which only reflects the inside anyway.

We can individuate from everything around us to do this. Let self-doubt up and go through it to the place of no doubt.

The world is our prayer mat when we let it be our prayer mat.

There are no guarantees as to how things are going to turn out. We need only turn out for the scene presenting itself at this time.

"There is no God who punishes us, what punishes us is our belief that God punishes us."

To do life we must go through periods of being totally
by ourselves ... and be OK with it.

If we stay with our own center we'll be taken to the places where we need to be. To do this we need only stay out of other people's center, that's enough.

We are everyone– all the prophets, saints, beggars and kings. We can be any one of these. We can take what we need from the world and leave the rest. To do this we must go through periods of being totally by ourselves. When we are totally with ourselves we are with all knowledge.

We must individuate to expand into who we already are.

The longer we can stay in true silence the more we can experience ourselves as silent.

Faith in ourselves allows us to experience faith in ourselves.

"There is no God who punishes us, what punishes us is our belief that God punishes us."

We don't own the scenes– we do the scenes, if you get what I mean.

Silence

The longer we keep our story in silence, the more powerful it becomes when we speak it.

Within us is everything we need. We stay in that place by not anticipating the future. This takes faith and fortitude– the deep inner belief that we are basically okay and that our life here is unfolding.

It's a fine balance between action and inaction. We can be active and quiet at the same time.

Every scene is a story. We need not accept anyone else's view of the story– except our own. It's all here for us to experience.

Everywhere we are is forever. Where we are now is forever and we are forever.

When we accept success as our mode, then we have purpose and direction in life. Individuation means we will not necessarily get agreement from the world.

We are telling this story to ourselves.

If you're always relating to the world, you're not relating to yourself enough.

"Within inactivity lies activity, and within activity lies inactivity. This is balance."

Individuation leads us to our own life. We must periodically remove ourselves from groups that have a consensus of opinion in order to experience our own consensus of opinion.

The mind plays out reels that are the mind's reals, and you know what? They're not real for us unless we make them real for us.

Multiple realities are where it's at.

The characters in our life come from within us. We gave birth to them and we can eliminate them from positions of importance in our lives if, and when, we choose to do so.

However we experience God, that's God.

Inspection is the road to our higher selves, not projection.

> "Within inactivity lies activity, and within activity lies inactivity. This is balance."

Balancing

Pay attention to where you are, not where you want to be. Then you'll be where you want to be.

It's not all going to blow up, we need only show up. Want love from others? Get it from yourself first, that's what original love is all about.

The outside does not move, we move.

The last scene dies hardest, and we get to choose when the last scene is up for us. What the world thinks it knows, it doesn't! The less serious we take ourselves, the less serious things are to us.

No need to worry about anything, every scene is on time.

We don't need to be active in other people's lives; their lives are their lives.

"The longer we keep our story in silence, the more powerful it becomes when we speak it."

Listen to the world, and you'll define who you are not.

When we let each person have their own reality, there is

more freedom for us; we're letting things happen.

Work on what is outside. Be quiet on the inside– that's how we learn about ourselves.

Is this for real? It's a sure deal. When we allow ourselves to feel.

Anything can happen. It does, you know. The thing is to do your own thing. We don't have to get anywhere. We are already there. Be modest. Then the gift is ours to give.

"The longer we keep our story in silence, the more powerful it becomes when we speak it."

No Blame

We need to expectorate our expectations. Aspirate our aspirations, and not exaggerate our exasperations.

Don't doubt about how things will turn out then we'll have more clout. Have no doubt about things turning out just how they turn out. No blame. We are here to believe our truth, our truth is who we are. Once upon a time we thought our truth (who we were) was not okay ... so we became someone else. When we thought and experienced that we were unacceptable, we felt our hearts break. We then protected our heart with ideas, beliefs, and maneuvers to prevent ourselves from feeling that hurt. Move forward and diffuse those ideas, beliefs, and maneuvers, by trusting the scenes in our process, and letting them come forward, and feel, and let it be. All space is sacred when we are in that place of sacredness.

"What the world says about things, is just that: sayings about things, which may not have anything to do with us right now. What is happening right now can be silent within silence, which is real science."

What the world extols, it also controls. We need only go

to our inner scrolls, and see what unrolls.

What excites the world, ignites, and, then takes flight. Why not go to the height, where there is no excite or flight?

Let the mysterious be the mysterious. This is the only thing that will quiet what is to be quieted and expand what is to be expanded. Then, we know that we have landed and aren't stranded or branded. Instead, are handed what we really need by that seed within the seed of our being.

It is never commanded that we are co-manned. This is our flight, so what is the fright? Show your might to yourself. Be in charge of your own journey. This is not a tourney of who is the best, leave that to the rest.

"What the world says about things, is just that: sayings about things, which may not have anything to do with us right now. What is happening right now can be silent within silence, which is real science."

Are Things Going Too Slow?

Reeling off the reels of our life– realing off the reals of our life.

We are dreaming this life; it is not real the way the world says it's real. When we allow ourselves the experience of being an outsider then we can go inside and be an insider. We don't have to be a hider.

Tomorrow will take care of itself.

The scenes we go through are what we want to bring out, so that we can be with ourselves.

What you think happened didn't happen the way you think it happened.

What you see in your dream, what does it mean? Stick around and see.

We have to let it all go and get on with the show even though it seems to be going too slow. It's all show biz.

"We need to expectorate our expectations. Aspirate our aspirations, and not exaggerate our exasperations."

Our path is our path. Don't be afraid to see what you've

chosen as your path from a point of individuality. It is your originality.

Everything is unbelievable until it becomes believable.

As we realize– we're alive.

Give all your love in each scene, there's plenty to go around.

You can't leave the world, that's not part of the deal. Go further into the real.

Open yourself up to life and life will open itself up to you.

We can make things happen when we let go of trying to make things happen.

You can't get back what once was. What was is not happening now. Each now is an improvement on the previous now, if we let it be news from the now.

> "We need to expectorate our expectations. Aspirate our aspirations, and not exaggerate our exasperations."

Don't worry about your impact on others, make a pact to impact yourself. If you really want to impact others, impact yourself. Let others do the same for themselves.

Surprise

Take credit for nothing, then we will be given credit for everything.

Don't take refuge in the reality of the world. Take refuge in the reality that you are experiencing, that is the only reality for you. Believe it! No one else can do that for you.

Don't try to do what is not yet doable.

"Courage is a willingness to go into the next scene, which is the next clue into you."

There's not always a need to display anger. Display curiosity, which is one of the gateways through anger.

We are protected from that which we think we are unprotected. We are a detective, not necessarily defective, and we are elected to be here now.

Everything is a surprise. That's what makes life interesting. Having expectations cancels out the element of surprise and what's possible.

When we think we know what's going to happen, it limits the game, and we get into blame and shame.

Worry comes when we think we know what's going to happen. Worry comes from the old set of beliefs about the self– limiting beliefs imposed by the tribe! It's really all about bringing up our creativity and choosing to take on another way of being. Our natural state is to be creative beings.

Individuation is really the first step in realizing the uniqueness of our life process– that our process is our life and as we allow ourselves to follow our life/process. That's what makes life an adventure.

"Courage is a willingness to go into the next scene, which is the next clue into you."

Courage

It takes courage to step out of the tribal paradigm and into our own process. Once we begin to unplug our identity from the tribe, we develop the faith and trust in our life to continue the unplugging.

The personal process always works, if we allow ourselves passion. The jam-up is not believing in our personal passion.

It's all about letting go of the choices from earlier on in our process and creating new ones.

Our process is our life. Our life is our process. We can't stop it. So let's go with it. It's here for us. We're here for us. We're not here for the tribe.

"Take credit for nothing, then we will be given credit for everything."

The bottom line is that we invite more possibilities into our life as we let go of old tribal restrictions concerning creativity and loyalty to previous experiences. The loyalty is always supported by fear of being excluded from the tribe.

We have been trained to think that we have to take our

cues from the routines of others– we don't have to. We need only take the cues from ourselves. We can do this by tuning into our feelings. Routines require us to not tune into our feelings; this is what keeps the routines going.

To keep ourselves going we need only honor our feelings and where we are with them. A big part of individuation is this process of differentiating how we feel as distinguished from how the tribe would want us to feel in order to fulfill its program.

There is no mystery greater than the mystery of our life. Don't anticipate, participate! Don't shift the scene before the scene shifts.

The more we see, the more we become present to see.

Don't join fear, adjourn fear to the rear, and stay in your gear.

"Take credit for nothing, then we will be given credit for everything."

The mind is a worrier, and a ruminator, and is mainly useful for gathering information about the world of illusion.

In life, as we grow older, we are actually getting better. Life is actually a process of healing, not of dying. As soon as we jump out of the here and now, we are out of the process of living.

We never have to worry about what to do next– it is always there for us to do next.

The Book of Revelations

We can build a support team for ourselves. It is made up of all the parts of us.

Time is never really stretched out, it just is what it is at every moment.

Every scene is set up by us so that we can handle it. There is no need to worry about what we don't have—we have what we need for now. In the next scene we'll have what we need for that scene. Know what I mean?

We never miss a scene we are destined to take part in, and we never take part in a scene we are destined to miss. Hmmmmmm.

There really is only one scene. It just seems to be broken up into separate scenes. This is what integration is all about.

The Book of Revelations is being written right now! Others' revelations are just that, others' revelations.

As we integrate, we detach, and breakdown the illusion of reality, and we experience that we are not being broken down. All pain comes from our identification with that which we feel is being broken down.

This book has come about as a result of our individual journeys through the quagmires of family and onto the path of self-discovery and joy. For those interested in finding out who they can really be, and have felt the feelings of their earlier life, we write this book.

The more we let ourselves experience that we don't know what is going on, the more we get to really see what is going on.

"We need to honor our impatience to experience our patience."

Being available to others is easy. Being available to ourselves is even easier. When we grow into this realization we actually get to experience our life as easier.

Core paradigm: "It's not fair." This can really jam us up, and prevent us from seeing and experiencing what is up for us, as it comes up for us.

> "We need to honor our impatience to experience our patience."

"It's not good to be impatient" another paradigm and another paradox. By accepting our impatience we get in touch with our patience.

What's Happening?

Don't expect anything in particular to happen and you will get to experience what is happening as it is happening.

Time really has nothing to do with us. When we don't project into the future, time becomes less of a factor to us. The issue of time always has to do with expectations. Expectations have to do with feeling that we are not good enough right now. Don't ignore your expectations because they will tell you a lot about yourself. Expectations are only expectations; they are not wrong. When we experience our life as falling apart we can then allow ourselves to feel that things are actually coming together. A new way of experiencing our being, operating outside the tribal thinking. We are all here together. We can't see ourselves until we see that we are all connected, and we are connected by love of all kinds. When we think we know what is going on we're just doing that for our own entertainment.

Wisdom is within awareness, and awareness is within wisdom. Try that one on for size.

When we aren't invested in making something happen

we actually leave space for something to happen with awareness. Life opens up to us when we open ourselves to it— it really is like that.

"We can build a support team for ourselves. It is made up of all the parts of us."

Self-acceptance of that which is unacceptable about ourselves leads to wisdom. This is a great paradox.

The tribe's take on things is off. It's as simple as that when we allow ourselves to be aware. When we let go of the tribe's take, and start to honor our own experience and feelings we get to reclaim ourselves.

> "We can build a support team for ourselves. It is made up of all the parts of us."

Mysterious Isn't It?

Don't pursue things, let them pursue you. Be receptive to what you are presenting to yourself; don't force things. The less we force things the more force they have as we imbibe them.

Maybe it's not about answers, but about experience.

Being with others is easy. Being with yourself is even easier.

There are no what if's. There is only what is right now. We are presenting scenes to ourselves as we need them to be presented. This is trust.

Don't support the world's efforts. Support your own.

Go into the fears of the known and experience the fearlessness of the unknown.

We really don't know why we are here. That's the great mystery of life.

"Bust the mind and trust the heart. The mind always wants a plan. What the mind thinks it knows it doesn't! The heart knows what it knows because it doesn't think about it."

We really have nothing to lose by being ourselves
in every scene. It's really as simple as that.

The more energy we put into any single image of ourselves, the farther away we are from ourselves. We have many selves to draw from.

Our whole life is a mystery to be experienced as just that. We really don't know why we're here– until we know why we're here. It's that kind of mystery, which has no history.

Why do people like mysteries? Because they know instinctively that life is a mystery.

"Bust the mind and trust the heart. The mind always wants a plan. What the mind thinks it knows it doesn't! The heart knows what it knows because it doesn't think about it."

Trying to fix things just doesn't work. What does work is letting go of trying to fix things.

Life is a process of manifestation. Our work and joy is to go through these manifestations without getting caught. What catches us is our not wanting to go through the process with feeling and self awareness.

Being overly aware of what others are doing or not doing can be a royal pain in the butt.

Things Are Flipped Around

We don't need to convince anyone of anything. The more we try, the more we become enmeshed.

It's a trap that may be easier to get into than to get out of. Let go of the need to control. Rather, let it all unfold in its own time.

Whatever happens is the world of illusion, and what does not happen is the world of reality. When we go beyond what is happening and what is not happening, we are free.

When we get to know ourselves we get to know everyone.

When we give up envy of others we can actually do what we envy others for doing.

What has passed was for us, and what is now is for us. It doesn't have to be a chore nor a bore– it's just what's in store, and with that, we can keep moving toward the shore of our reality through– our duality.

"Maybe it's not about answers, but about experience."

Each time we experience and identify grace, it becomes

something greater than what we experienced before the door opened to that place of grace within grace.

Don't worry about tomorrow. Today, it doesn't pay. Tomorrow is just the next moment, and that is always cool, not cruel, unless we take on the victim role as a lifestyle, which is really a deathstyle.

> "Maybe it's not about answers, but about experience."

It all changes, when we allow it to change–otherwise, guess what? Nothing changes for us!

It's time for new material in this serial called our life. Greater awareness leads to greater capacity for choice, and this leads to greater awareness of our capacity for choice.

Guarantees are a tease, they can't please. They're as good as a sneeze, and just create a breeze.

The willingness to be impacted is the road to wisdom, and wisdom is the road to being impacted.

I am what I am, and I accept what I am– everything else can scram.

Don't make a big deal out of what is not a big deal!

It's All Done With Mirrors

Too much security actually leads to immaturity.

Direct your own play within the play of the world. It's all an act and a play being performed for our entertainment, not our detainment or restrainment.

There are different ways to get there, where we belong, it's like a song. We really can't go wrong as long as we remember why we came here, not to go insane but to make things plain, and then, reign over our own reign.

"Everything comes in its own time, and yet there really is no such thing as time– figure that one out!"

The more we experience ourselves as deserving, the more we get to experience what we have reserved for ourselves.

Those who claim to know– don't.

It's good to lead our life with the realization that we may never see the scene that we think we have to see. We are just itinerant, travelling actors on the stage of illusion.

Let the world come to you– it will.

The less we want from a scene, the more we will get from a scene.

Want to be a poet? Realize that you don't know it.

If you take people where they're at, you won't have a spat.

Be on the trail of your own discovery, no need to be in a state of recovery. That's the real discovery. It's all research.

The mind can make you blind to what you have right now. Since we have used our mind to connect with our distorted notions/beliefs, we need only open our eyes to what is around us right now. We can learn how to use the mind, for our empowerment.

There are no models– we are posing for ourselves.

"Everything comes in its own time, and yet there really is no such thing as time– figure that one out!"

Real Adventure

Don't try to change what is not changeable. It will change when the time comes!

This is not about God. It is about us manifesting as God. It's not God's story, it's our story. If we want to realize God's story we must realize our story; then the two are one.

The moment is real, the projections are not. We need to go through the unreal to the real. This is awareness.

We can treat life as interesting and as real as we want to. Life is a venture into more venture. This is adventure!

We don't know what's going to happen, and we don't know what's not going to happen. Try figuring that one out.

"Too much security actually leads to immaturity."

Life is about individuation not incineration.

Stop looking for cues as to what comes next. It'll come when it comes. This is called patience. We can only create our own future, we can't create it with someone else. This is individuation.

When we don't have a lot of questions about why things are happening or not happening, then things happen through the whole range. We don't have to arrange things to happen. We just have to let go of seeing ourselves as the arranger.

What's right for you is not necessarily right for another person. Don't try to influence other people, influence yourself. That's the best influence.

Live happily ever after right now.

"Too much security actually leads to immaturity."

Why pick up the worries of others? We can't do it for them. It's not our part to impart.

If you seek an ally's wisdom, then take that wisdom and use it.

The best theater is the theater of your life. Whatever you think it is, it isn't anyway.

Arriving By Not Striving

What has passed, is in time. What is happening right now is out of time. Our goal is to be out of time.

Things shift as we let more in, from that place of wisdom within, which, lightens up what is without.

Don't have patience with the world. Have patience with yourself, that's enough.

Things seem to end, and then they start again.

No need to compete for the scene, just be for the scene.

> "Hold onto your center. Especially when you are with those you consider close to you– this can be put in the warning category."

Every morning we get a new script from the script department ... wherever that is. There's no use trying to look ahead in the script. It's not written yet, until we get there. In the meantime stay in character.

Take advantage of life don't let life take advantage of you.

When you see karma then you see obstacles, stop seeing karma, and you'll stop seeing obstacles. So much for karma.

You don't have to be a donkey, and carry wisdom to others, just let it transform you. That's enough!

"Hold onto your center. Especially when you are with those you consider close to you– this can be put in the warning category."

It's all improvisational! Let your expectations go and then, on with the show! Seeing life as a threat? Nyet! Things are simply not going to work out the way you think. So, be in sync. That's all!

Each scene is exquisitely timed to arrive at the time we need it to arrive. No need to strive, just be alive to arrive.

Want to let go? All you need to do is not be so attached to your history. After all, it's still all a mystery.

What the world proclaims as greatness isn't.

Striving is just conniving. It doesn't lead to arriving.

Clarity

Bring into focus that which will serve you, and leave that which will unnerve you.

We came here with many allies. As our awareness expands, so does our experience of these allies.

There are no catastrophes! It's only the next scene.

If you insist on being in a lousy mood then you'll be in a lousy mood. It's better to be in a reasonable mood with yourself.

What's going on in your head isn't what's really going on!

If you wait until everything's perfect before you're free, you'll never get to be the way you want to be.

"Don't try to change what is not changeable. It will change when the time comes!"

Each moment begins anew, so jump into the brew and be you.

Don't expect anything, and you'll get everything you need to be you right now.

Different people have different ways of getting it. Let 'em be.

If you give yourself a revelation, then you're also giving yourself support for that revelation. There's no need to get caught by how others are doing it or not doing it. Mind your own business.

Faith is to play out a scene when you don't know why.

Rackets are our karma drop the rackets; along goes the karma.

The bizarre scenes? They can often teach us the most.

No one knows what we go through. All we need to do is go through.

Let everything pass through us, it's not designed to screw us.

"Don't try to change what is not changeable. It will change when the time comes!"

Tribal Vision Is Tribal Vision

The more we are with our own reality, the less we need to take on.

As we go through our feelings and our thoughts, we get to our feelings and thoughts.

When you let someone into your life it's like school.

What is unrealistic? If it's happening for you ... then it's realistic!

The tribe calls it optimistic ... call it an attitude with possibilities. Optimistic is static; possibility is open-ended ... it can grow and change. The tribe doesn't like that ... it always wants to freeze things.

We find ourselves asking, "What do I want?" Where did we learn that? It's so final! But, "What do I want now?" That sounds okay!

"We must all go from just surviving the moment to actually enjoying the moment."

We're always finding out what we want! In fact, that's why we're here in this life! To find and experience what we want!!!!!!

It's what we really want ... and it comes from our core. And the way we do that is to find our own rhythm. It's a specific pace that is lovingly and biologically designed for us ... so that we can find and experience our core in our own time.

Goals and plans are okay. They exist in the future where our present life does not yet exist. We need to always be alive. So we can move into the present with the practice of vision!

Vision expands, changes and exists in the present. The present becomes the future and the future is always right now.

Our vision is our creativity. Through our vision we actively involve ourselves in our creative unfolding. We can't have vision from our past and vision certainly does not exist in the future; it is here in the moment where creativity lies.

"We must all go from just surviving the moment to actually enjoying the moment."

Creativity

We take the moment for granted. It is a powerful point in time. Not only do we create from this place; we also get to experience how we feel.

When we have feelings that have negative implications we get jammed-up thinking that we are doomed, and we'll be like this forever! Well, the moment is forever! So, if it's a feeling that we don't embrace we find ourselves in fear and/or judgment, this is what being jammed up is all about.

Our creative process is about our life, and, how it unfolds.

When we have faith in our life, it naturally teaches us to be responsible for what comes. Not blame!! Just responsible, "This is my life, this is what's happening."

Maybe we're only experiencing hardships and disaster from the tribal point of view.

"The more we are with our own reality, the less we need to take on."

It's all a tapestry of experiences for us to give our creative process richness, depth and many leads toward

It's all right to be whoever you want to be for right now.

what we came here to do, which is exactly what we are doing right now, for now and later. We'll see.

Thinking about the future? Don't bother! It's not what you think anyway.

It's alright to be whoever you want to be for right now.

To remember is to re-member.

Take a risk! Really want something? So bad that you are willing to die to your old self, which is everything that you have experienced up to now so far! This is letting go.

"The more we are with our own reality, the less we need to take on."

Scared?

If you're not scared, you ain't getting repaired.

It's not about becoming right; it's about becoming clear. What we have been taught to think of as right may not be right, in fact, for us at this point in our life.

People who remind us of what is right for us are just talking. Nobody is where we're at no matter how much they think they are. This is what individuation is all about.

There is no place to get back to or to get to. We're already there, where we need to be. This is self acceptance.

The only model we have is ourselves ... what we feel ... what we dream, and our desires. This is unique; there is no comparison. Being busy is okay. Better to be aware.

Anything that we compare ourselves to is not us.

Any time we go to a meeting it's always with ourselves.

Be creative in everything you do.

"Make no mistake about it, things do change. Our life

is about change if we stay open to it."

What a therapist needs to do is to do what he or she is asking the patient to do; show them how to be real by being real themselves. Everything else is what it is.

When we learn to communicate with ourselves, guess what? We can talk to and listen to everyone, if we choose to.

Take the burden off of yourself; that is your job. Want to cure someone? Cure yourself first; it's a lot easier. Our business is to follow our own business.

Whatever you're thinking, forget it! That's the only way to get it! Why keep something alive in your head if it isn't alive now?

"Make no mistake about it, things do change. Our life is about change if we stay open to it."

When you're stripped away of yourself, as you think you know it to be, then you get to re-ally be with yourself as you really are right now. That's always okay and that's self confidence.

Choice

We really do have a choice as to how we are going to play out the scene no matter what form it comes in. This is a great secret that we have to reveal to ourselves and the choice is always a great secret for us to realize, believe and feel safe with. Remember, we only have to save ourselves. All other beings have to save themselves.

Applaud yourself!

Let wisdom kick into action whenever you want to be here now.

Within our precious heart lies the nurturance of wisdom which is grace. To taste that grace we need only keep pace with what is up for us.

The balance for our life is to be proactive while letting the scene come to you. That balance is our wisdom. This is how we change our life.

The wisdom of our life comes in what appears to be strange ways; but it does come.

"If you're not scared, you ain't getting repaired."

We all have to figure this out for ourselves. That's

individuation.

Take what comes and go with it.

If you give up trying to control a situation then you are open to get what you need. The situation only serves as the catalyst which is not real in and of itself.

Let things come to you. It's more fun.

Everything in its own time; now that's sublime.

The thing is to feel the feelings and not be attached to them. This does take practice, that's a good program.

If you're thinking of something and you really don't want to do it, don't! Do something else; then what you thought you wanted to do will look different and you can experience it from a new perspective.

Dignity is often about not doing something rather than doing something.

"If you're not scared, you ain't getting repaired."

Creativity seems to have something to do with the willingness to be alone, I mean really alone for periods of time, and be all right with it.

Do Yourself a Favor

It's alright to feel anger. It can serve you as a high test fuel and you don't have to act like a fool.

Don't feel what others are feeling, feel what you're feeling. It's a lot easier and much more satisfying.

Stay with your creativity! It goes hand in hand with your process.

Don't pursue things. Let them pursue you!

Not doing something can often give you more awareness than if you did it. What is within awareness is personal power and what is within personal power is awareness.

It's good to individuate without finding fault with other beings. It keeps the slate clear.

"The greatest favor that we can do for anyone is to let them be free to be who they need to be, not who we need them to be. Some might call this love."

Being the center of attention isn't so great. Better to stay with your attention in your own center of attention.

Don't pursue things, let them pursue you.

If you're afraid to do something, guess what? Don't do it! It's okay to be afraid; just wait until the fear passes. You can choose from a clearer space whether or not you really want to do the thing or not.

Take back all of your projections and allow yourself to be empowered by them. This is how we gain back awareness of our power.

Everything we see, experience and believe is a projection of our own reality. If we stick with our own reality, there will be no duality.

Stay out of the disaster mode and you'll stay out of disaster.

Might as well have some fun playing your part from the start. You don't have to do everything perfectly. It's just not that way. You really don't know what's going to happen next. It's just that way.

> "The greatest favor that we can do for anyone is to let them be free to be who they need to be, not who we need them to be. Some might call this love."

Want something to do? Try relaxing. It really does work you know.

Want something to worry about? Try not worrying! If we've called up a scene, that alone, indicates that we are prepared to handle it

Ask for What You Want

Everything that we do is just another way of healing. Our work is to just stay with the feeling, that's how we do the healing!

All feelings are the same; it's we who give them a name.

Guidance is coming our way; we need only to be open to it.

It's a blessing to be alive today and every day that comes our way.

From within silence comes our creativity.

"Within inactivity lies activity, and within activity lies inactivity. This is balance."

"It's alright to feel anger. It can serve you as a high test fuel and you don't have to act like a fool."

Live one day at a time and you will live one day at a time.

Pray to God for guidance and you will get it from yourself! What a wonder.

It's all a dream. Know what I mean? Everyone has to

take care of themselves– okay?

There is no place to go to except to you.

Take the focus off the other person and put the focus on you. That's how we stay out of other people's stuff, and be with our own!

Want someone to talk to? Talk to yourself! There's nothing wrong with that. Speaking to others as you would speak to yourself? That's easy.

There's nothing else that you should be doing, except what you're doing and, you know what? You don't have to do that forever if you don't want to.

Talking to others is the same as talking to yourself– in a different way.

"It's alright to feel anger. It can serve you as a high test fuel and you don't have to act like a fool."

Further Into the Mystery

Talking to yourself is the same as talking to others in a different way.

Who's got Mother issues? Everyone who's breathing that's who and the same goes for Dad issues.

Don't feel others' pain; feel your own pain. That's how you gain trust in yourself.

Don't worry about examining the nature of God. Experience the nature of man and woman– it's more real because you get to feel and that makes you more real to deal with yourself as you emerge from that place of inner awareness, which is manifesting right now.

Who goes from scene to scene? You, that's who goes from scene to scene to be seen. By yourself.

Can't figure out what's going on? Good! Because we can't figure it out! If we try we come up dry, better to stay with what you are doing now, and let that transform you, which will then be what's up for you. Each moment has a different revelation for us to partake in.

Getting things done? It's all the same– little things

or big things. Make them all little things. That's perspective.

Seek comfort from yourself, not from others. Their work is to comfort themselves.

We can make the big things little by promoting them in importance– this is how we can take care of things. A real paradox.

We can't solve and end this mystery so we might as well keep the mystery going.

"What is seen is just scenery."

"What is seen is just scenery."

It's all a lie, so don't believe any of it. Better to smile at it.

True discipline most often has to do with not doing something rather than doing something.

Everyday is a new life. Treat it that way. You never know when the last scene will come or if there will even ever be a last scene. That's the mystery of life.

What Is Doing Anyway?

You can't do anything about that which you can't do anything about.

Tell yourself that you're okay and you will be okay. Okay?

No more waiting; there's nothing to wait for.

Let your process be your best friend.

It's easy when you just play your part from the start, and the heart, and now each moment is a new start.

We can change the rules for ourselves whenever we want to and you know what? That changes the rules also for those we interact with. It works that way. Don't be afraid to be alive.

"Everything that we do is just another way of healing. Our work is to just stay with the feeling, that's how we do the healing!"

Planning for the future? Don't! There isn't any the way we think it is anyway.

How can anyone know what we go through? When we

don't even know ourselves what we're going through because it's not in the realm of knowing, it's in the realm of experiencing not knowing and being alright with that experience of not knowing. This is a key point folks.

The world looks to knowing. Better to look to not knowing. Within not knowing is knowing that's a great secret for us to know.

When the world ceases to attract us, or distract us, we're not there to be attracted or distracted.

If you think you saw something then you did see something then.

"Everything that we do is just another way of healing. Our work is to just stay with the feeling, that's how we do the healing!"

Want to know about people? Know yourself.

You never did make a mistake you know! And you never will.

You never really know what's going to happen next. So why bother yourself worrying about it? It's never what you think.

Thinking?

Whatever you think another person is thinking about, they're not thinking about what you think they're thinking about.

Everyday we can clear the slate and start anew. We can do that for ourselves.

It's alright to step out of line and feel fine.

It's all about staying with uncertainty.

Don't take responsibility for what another person wants or experiences. Take the responsibility for what you want and experience.

Go into the tribal beliefs and escape with your own take on things.

Nothing is real to us until it becomes real to us and that takes being real.

Don't carry your thoughts around. They're too heavy.

"Don't take responsibility for what another person wants or experiences. Take the responsibility for what you want and experience."

Whatever you think another person is thinking about,
they're not thinking about what you think. They're thinking
about what they're thinking about.

Just because you're thinking it doesn't mean you gotta do it. Maybe you're just thinking about it.

Wanting something allows you to let go of it and that's a really good practice.

Whatever you treat sacredly will reveal it's sacredness to you, especially yourself.

Never mind what others think about you. Just be you and think about what you want to think about you.

The usual affect of the tribal paradigms or any other paradigm is to influence or define our behavior. Shift awareness and be with personal creativity. It can instantly expand, change and recreate any paradigm.

"Don't take responsibility for what another person wants or experiences. Take the responsibility for what you want and experience."

When you're in your head, feeling overwhelmed and confused, don't try to think about how to get out of your head. Get out of thinking about it and just be amused at thinking.

Resolve

Life is exciting when we're a witness in the scene which is up for us right now.

Each experience is amazing and sacred when we're in the moment and it's always the moment.

Scared is the other side of sacred and sacred is the other side of scared. It's up to you. Wanna be scared? That's up to you too.

"If you walk around feeling that there is no fear, then guess what? You won't go to that place where fear exists. If you walk around letting yourself go into that place where fear exists, and go through it, then you will be free."

Doubt is the feeling that you didn't do something right or aren't doing something right, wrong! Doubt is something you go into and come out of. That's all. Don't put meaning into it since it only exists if you allow it to exist and it only exists within fear. So if you stay with fear you stay with doubt and that's okay too.

Go into fear and doubt and come out of fear and doubt.

You can plan the day. That's okay. Better to expand the

day by not planning too much, then something can happen if you allow it to happen.

The greatest thing that you could do for someone is to let them go to that place that they need to go to. And don't annoy them too much on the way.

Take on what you want to take on, and let go of what you want to let go of– this is called balance, or yin/yang.

Today is the play of the day.

There is nothing to resolve, period! Now that's real resolve.

"If you walk around feeling that there is no fear, then guess what? You won't go to that place where fear exists. If you walk around letting yourself go into that place where fear exists, and go through it, then you will be free."

The Guru is You

As we begin to give ourselves permission to experience how we feel we can then explore the feelings. No pressure to change anything!! Just honor what is present. Through this exploration we can discover other manifestations of our expression, i.e., confusion. I thought that I was feeling confusion but; as I explored how I felt I identified other feelings other than being confused. I was merely experiencing the newness of being in the unknown. Since being in the unknown is an unacceptable state for the tribal thinking, this will usually trigger a reaction of confusion. Real confusion is not honoring how you feel even the feeling of being numb and that's okay too.

It's all an act– none of it is in fact.

Respect the guru in yourself and lighten up!

There is no hindsight, only present sight.

There aren't many moments; there is only one moment.

If you're nobody, then guess what? You're somebody and being alive is being somebody and being nobody is also being somebody.

The thing is to see when the secure has become the prison. Sometimes we need prison to learn about ourselves.

The way it is happening is the way it is happenin' for now.

There is no right way to do this life!

No need to rush or mull— that makes life a bit dull.

"A man can feel a woman's strength in himself and a woman can feel a man's strength in herself. That is balance in life."

"A man can feel a woman's strength in himself and a woman can feel a man's strength in herself. That is balance in life."

It's a Mind-Blower

There's absolutely no relationship between what we think is happening and what is actually happening. Isn't that amazing?

Thinking never has to do with what's really happening! It just has to do with thinking, period. We actually have very little to do with our own thinking. Now isn't that amazing?

You never have to do things as fast as you think you just have to do them.

It's best to have no intention. Then you can pay attention to paying attention to your intention.

One minute things look like this, and the next minute they look like that. They're both right for the time they appear and then they disappear. Hmmmmmmm.

Another tribal take: be careful of what you ask for! You know, it's really alright to ask for what you want, who's to say not.

"Stop seeing everything as miracles, and guess what? You get to experience everything as miracles."

You never really left your home to come here to this place. You are still there and here at the same time. So, where's here and where's there?

Lead an outrageous life, what the hell!

You can interpret things the way you want to interpret them, which is anyway you want to.

You really don't have to do what you think you have to do and you don't have to do what you don't want to, or do anything for that matter. Just keep breathing, for starters.

"Stop seeing everything as miracles, and guess what? You get to experience everything as miracles."

Ahhhhhhh another thing not to worry or do anything about. That's how we clear out space to breathe life into the next moment.

When you really think about it, everything that is happening is a mind blower.

Humor and Passion

Bust the mind and trust the heart. The mind always wants a plan. What the mind thinks it knows it doesn't! The heart knows what it knows because it doesn't think about knowing.

Everything comes in its own time, and yet there really is no such thing as time– figure that one out!

Hold onto your center. Especially when you are with those you consider close to you– this can be put in the warning category.

We must all go from just surviving the moment to actually enjoying the moment.

Make no mistake about it, things do change. Our life is about change if we stay open to it.

What is seen is just scenery.

Stop seeing everything as miracles, and guess what? You get to experience everything as miracles.

"Life is exciting when we're a witness in the scene which is up for us right now."

We're writing our own story as we go along.

It's alright to let your heart shatter. It really doesn't matter. What matters is that we allow our hearts to be shattered and experience what matters.

Life is a mystery! No sense getting lost in our history. It's just for study which can really be fun, if we play it with humor and passion. This is your story; this is your history.

"Life is exciting when we're a witness in the scene which is up for us right now."

The fact that anything can happen at any time means that it is not in our control. So why try to control what is not controllable?

It is all up for grabs. So why grab for that which is not up for you yet?

Answers

There are no answers– there is only wisdom.

There is no tomorrow not today.

Talk less and listen more. Thank you!

Whatever the tribe's take on things, forget it!

The way to get what you want is to let go of what you want. Now that's a real paradox; the tribe doesn't get that one at all!

We really have nothing to lose by being ourselves in every scene– it's really as simple as that.

People say: "With my bad luck?" Wrong!

It's the mind that feels abandoned. It feels abandoned when actually we're just being ourselves.

That's all that's happening and when we do that there is no fear there and we get to experience that and remember what's possible during this birth.

Each moment is different– that's what it's all about.

There is nowhere to get to. Just be here now that's how

we do it.

It's all up for grabs. Don't believe anything they say! There are no mistakes.

"We're writing our own story as we go along."

No one really knows what waiting is all about. There's nothing to wait for– it's already here, what we need.

You never know what's going to happen until it happens. Most or all of what is called living is "lived" in the future or projected future. Isn't it strange that all of the real substance of living exists in the present?

> "We're writing our own story as we go along."

What If?

There are no what if's, only what is present for you right now, and that keeps changing.

Honor the work you do and you honor yourself.

Thinking about the past and thinking about the future is thinking about what is not happening, why bother.

Duty is not duty until it is experienced as not duty! It's all about duty to ourselves anyway!

Every experience is something we call up from within. That's no sin to serve ourselves. That's how we serve others.

If you find yourself worrying, don't worry about it. The world is a mad house. The only thing that matters is love.

Art saves lives.

Go right within the middle of fear and experience yourself as a fearless person.

"It's alright to let your heart shatter. It really doesn't matter. What matters is that we allow our hearts to be shattered and experience what matters."

Why wonder about things? Everything is a wonder!

Do what you really want to do, why not! What the hell! What the world says ain't what it says it is. Why not you say what it is.

Religions are all flipped around– they take people away from their real spirituality. It's best to stay away from them. They have nothing to do with who we really are. It's better to believe in ourselves rather than what religion says about it.

What we've done is not who we are and what we think we have done is all in our head anyway.

What is going on for us right now is what is going on for us right now!

> "It's alright to let your heart shatter. It really doesn't matter. What matters is that we allow our hearts to be shattered and experience what matters."

Making It Easy

Be your own independent film channel.

Honor every part of your life, no matter what form it takes.

Everything is really here for us right now. You don't have to do what everyone else is doing. Just do what you're doing.

We are not our history– that's the mystery!

It's not what they say!

"There are no answers– there is only wisdom!"

Things don't happen the way you think they're happening, or will happen, or even have happened. Try to make sense out of that one! It doesn't make any sense; so give that one up. That's all we can do– it's really quite easy when we decide to make it easy on ourselves.

Stop looking for angels out there! They're here! Right now see if you can see them here.

Don't worry about later now! In the now there is no later. Be with what is up for you now, and it becomes later. Don't worry about now. There is no later. Remember! You can't figure it out– just live it with humor and gusto.

We're not acting for them! We're acting for ourselves– got it?

Time is ours to do with what we want to do with it. We have that choice to choose or not choose– that is the question! To be is to choose to be alive. This is creativity.

"There are no answers– there is only wisdom!"

Play one scene at a time.

Everyone's take on reality is their take on reality.

Creation

There are no parameters to the borders of despair.
When we go there we can repair the borders of despair
and create new boundaries for ourselves. This is how we
can feel the experience of safety and the freedom and
expansiveness of our spirit– which is our life here and
now as it unfolds for us with passion from our hearts.

Take the time to create your own life. Don't worry
about how others are creating theirs. Pay attention to
your own creation.

Nothing that happens really makes any sense – so what!

People say: "You're fooling yourself!" Wrong! There
is no way that we can fool ourselves– better to school
ourselves.

Dreams come true as they come true for you. This is
true. It is all a dream to be dreamt. We are not exempt.
This is our part for now.

"Life is a mystery! No sense getting lost in our history.
It's just for study which can really be fun, if we play it
with humor and passion. This is your story; this is your
history."

The mind is always reminding us of what is not happening. How about focusing in on what is happening.

Tell yourself who you are. Ask yourself who am I? And then answer yourself in any way you want.

Life is not under our control– unless we give up the idea that life is under our control! Forget it and get on with things as they unfold. That's being bold, and for that we're never too old. As we enjoy that awareness we actually become younger! How's that for a paradigm shift?

We are responsible to ourselves, not to others!

"Life is a mystery! No sense getting lost in our history. It's just for study which can really be fun, if we play it with humor and passion. This is your story; this is your history."

Don't love another more than you love yourself. Withdraw and take back that projection– that's being alone with yourself! Then we don't give ourselves away to our projections."

Knowing

"Thou shalt not worship any God but me." Sound familiar? Everything is happening for you right now!

There is no mind! Take that projection back. Whatever needs attention for you, do it the way you want to do it. This is the other world you know. We don't need outside intervention from other beings. We can provide our own interventions by just being.

Don't look at what you've been through; look at what is in front of you.

You never know what you really know until you know it; then that changes.

Anything really is possible when you believe, and realize, and experience that anything is really possible.

"Be your own independent film channel."

Why look for things to do? Do what you're doing for now.

Everyone's a sufi; so treat them like that. Real silence comes from the place of real silence within the inner core of each person who is a sufi.

Start the day off with not knowing what's going to happen. That's good! It's true that people are somewhat nuts and they're also real sweet deep down and so are we.

Every day is a new day.

Nothing is really a big deal although it may feel that way– you're breathing aren't you?

"Be your own independent film channel."

If you're down and out then be with that. See where that takes you.

What Comes Next

What do you do after you've exhausted all possibilities? Do what you want to do until you don't want to do it anymore.

Whatever you're drawn to, go there and you know what? There is nowhere to go to where you are not there already.

Don't plan the future! It's okay to have visions until they lead to the next visions. Then we go beyond visions and dreams and plans, too. Right here now we can seek that paradise within.

It it's up for you, do it. If it's not up for you, then there is nothing for you to do about it.

It's alright to be discontent with what you've got in order to be content with what you've got.

"The fact that anything can happen at any time means that it is not in our control. So why try to control what is not controllable?"

Lightin up; healing comes through passion and humor; it's not as serious as they say.

Want to know what comes next? Guess what– there is no next. What's up now is all there is – for now anyway.

Want to know how you're doing? Ask yourself! Look in the mirror and ask yourself. You're the only one who knows how you feel and that's the only thing that counts. Feelings create action; action creates change.

It's a real paradox, if you back off, something happens that we can't even imagine.

What's life about? It's about what it's about, for right now anyway.

Deal with what's up for you or don't deal with it, and see what happens!

We don't really know what's going to happen; that's what makes life so amazing. Stay open to staying open to your life as it unfolds for you at this point in your life.

"The fact that anything can happen at any time means that it is not in our control. So why try to control what is not controllable?"

Here and Now

To be intimate and to be independent, that's the ticket to you.

Heal yourself and you heal the people. Mother Earth is here to support us.

If it matters to you, then that's an important enough reason for you to do it for yourself. And if it doesn't matter to you, then it doesn't matter to you.

Befriend the mind. It doesn't matter. It's just showing us its stuff. We don't have to buy unless we want to. Don't follow the mind's visions. Follow your own visions. The mind has no vision to speak of. We get to pick the visions we want to play in.

The situation doesn't produce the emotion that we feel. We produce the emotion so that we can deal with the situation. Actually we're covered in each scene; only we forget that sometimes.

There is no sooner, or later. There is only now.

Don't chase things. Embrace things. Especially your own life, then you can embrace others.

"It's all up for grabs. So why grab for that which is not up for you yet?"

Let life be a mystery. Then we can go beyond our history, which is also a mystery.

Inner peace has nothing to do with outer events. Actually events don't really matter until they appear for us as we call them up for ourselves.

None of us really knows how life works until we experience it directly through our heart where all knowing exists for us.

Things come out of nowhere and go back to nowhere, which is here now.

"It's all up for grabs. So why grab for that which is not up for you yet?"

Let Go

Whenever you feel desperate, take a respite from whatever is making you feel desperate.

As things open up, the unbelievable becomes believable.

When you've run out of options, that's when you open yourself up to new options.

Bathe yourself in your own grace.

At every moment our life can be light, the weight is everything from our past that we carry around.

> "Let go of anything that no longer serves you. Lightin up!"

"Let go of anything that no longer serves you. Lightin up!"

About the Author

After receiving his doctorate in psychology in 1969, Dr. Art Hochberg proved himself to be a dynamic teacher and innovator in the field of psychology. Within a year of receiving his degree, he became the Psychology department head at St. Mary's College in South Bend, Indiana, and also taught at Notre Dame University where he initiated several new courses and program changes toward the field of Humanistic Psychology. Dr. Hochberg was one of the earliest members of the Association for Humanistic Psychology, and gave several talks on the subject at their annual conference.

While continuing to develop his own ideas in the field over the next nine years, he taught experientially-oriented psychology courses, travelling in Uganda, Ceylon, Israel, and Switzerland, among other countries. All the while, he was deepening his spiritual focus. He visited religious centers, spent a year in a Zen Buddhist monastery and has spent thirty-nine years studying with the Sufi Master Bawa Muhaiyaddeen.

Dr. Hochberg's vision was transformative on an organizational level as well. Wherever he worked, it was common for him to revamp the institution's existing program, hire new staff, and take part in presenting the new program to the general public. Such examples in the late 70's include Urbana College in Ohio where he was the Division Chairman of Social Services; in Fort Dix, NJ, where he was the Clinical Director of the Drug and Alcohol Program, supervising 20 drug and alcohol counselors, developing treatment programs for the patients at Walson Army Hospital, and conducting seminars around the base for commanders, soldiers, and their dependents. In 1979 at the newly established Fordham-Page Clinic in Radnor, PA, Dr. Hochberg served as Clinical Director, responsible for counselor training, teaching nutrition, and presenting the clinic's holistically-oriented program to the public.

In the early 80's, Dr. Hochberg established his private practice. In the early years of his practice, he was known as a nutritional psychologist, since he was one of the few psychologists in the country at that time using nutrition in their practice. He appeared on television and was a radio guest numerous times speaking about the nutritional approach to the treatment of psychological problems. Several national magazines and newspapers also covered his groundbreaking work. He trained under such notable practitioners as Dr. Paavo Airola, a Finnish Nutritionist; Dr. John Christopher, a leading herbalist; and Dr. Carl Pfeiffer, who was the foremost orthomolecular psychiatrist at the time. Dr. Hochberg joined the International Academy of Preventive Medicine and spoke at several medical conferences about the role of Psychology and the body, appearing with Dr. Linus Pauling, and Dr. Jeffrey Bland, among others.

In addition, Dr. Hochberg had a practice at the Center for Preventive Medicine in Bala Cynwyd, Pennsylvania for eleven years, and published fifteen articles on stress and nutrition. In November, 1981, Prevention Magazine wrote a feature article about his work on nutrition as he combined it with Psychology which was included in Prevention's Complete Book of Vitamins in 1984. Dr. Hochberg also wrote a chapter in The Metabolic Management of Cancer — A Physicians Protocol and Reference Book. In 1993, he became the Director of the Holistic Health Program at Rosemont College in PA, and was also on the Adjunct Psychology faculty at Widener University.

He also worked as a prison psychologist in southern New Jersey, and in several outpatient mental health clinics in New Jersey and Pennsylvania.

Currently, Dr. Hochberg continues to maintain his own private practice as a licensed psychologist, and mainly deals with the transformational process that people can experience as they go through the various "changes" in their life. These "changes" serve as the Process for each individual's transformation, and greater self-awareness. In addition, Dr. Hochberg serves as an intake psychologist at a Philadelphia inner city mental health clinic. He has written several articles and pamphlets on

Transformational Psychology, a term which he coined, which transcends the scope of Transpersonal Psychology by addressing the core issues of our human existence as they are reflected in our daily spiritual life.

Dr. Art, "Letting Go!"

Other Dr. Art Books

LIGHTIN UP! is available at:

Amazon – Mobi format for Kindle and Mobipocket ereaders, and paperback.

Barnes & Noble – in EPUB format (usable on most ereaders with the exception of Kindle and Mobipocket), paperback and PDF.

Lulu Publishing – in EPUB format, paperback and PDF.

Apple iBookstore – in EPUB format and iBooks format. Both formats can be directly downloaded from the iPad.

LETTING GO is available at:

Amazon – Mobi format for Kindle and Mobipocket ereaders.

Barnes & Noble – in EPUB format (usable on most ereaders with the exception of Kindle and Mobipocket), paperback and PDF.

Lulu Publishing – in EPUB format, paperback and PDF.

Apple iBookstore – in EPUB format and iBooks format. Both formats can be directly downloaded from the iPad.